This Log Belongs To Captain:

_____

DEDICATION

This book is dedicated to all the energetic Boaters out there who want to keep record of their boat maintenance and each boating trip. .

You are my inspiration for producing books

and I'm honored to be a part of keeping all your Boating notes & records organized.

This journal notebook will help you record your details and experiences as you care for your boat and take boating outings.

Thoughtfully put together with these sections to record: Vessel Information, Engine Info, Generator Info, Expense Log, Boat Record Log and Photos.

HOW TO USE THIS BOOK:

The purpose of this book is to keep all of your Boating notes and trips all in one place. It will help keep you organized.

This Boat Log will allow you to accurately document every detail about your boat and also track your boating adventures. It's a great way to chart your course as Captain of the Ship.

Here are examples of the prompts for you to fill in and write about your experience in this book:

1. Vessel Information - Date of Purchase, Purchased From, Manufacturer, Model, Year Built, Builder, Designer, Hull #, Vessel Type, Class, Vertical Clearance, Hull Type.
2. Engine Information - Manufacturer, Model, Serial # Port, Engine Oil Type, Serial # Starboard, Engine HP, Engine Oil Capacity, Battery Model, Cruising RPM, Max RPM, Vertical Clearance, Hull Type.
3. Specific Information - Fuel Filter Mfg and Part #, Oil Filter Mfg and Part #, Spark Plug Brand and Part #, Water Pump Mfg and Part #, Impeller Kit Mfg and Part #.
4. Generator Information - Manufacturer, Model #, Serial #, Install Date, Oil Type, Oil Capacity, Oil Filter, Fuel Filter, Impeller Kit Mfg and Part #.
5. Expense Log - Write any expenses you have for maintenance. Date, Item, Purchased From, Price.
6. Boat Log Record - Details of each trip. Date & Time, Destination, Weather, Forecast, Wind, Visibility, Water Conditions, Length of Trip, My Crew, Passengers, Marinas/ Ports Visited, Memories: for writing any important details about your trip such as did you go fishing and what fish you caught, any story or drawings, was the trip a success, what useful patterns did you notice, any activities you did, will you go back there in the future, diving, etc.
7. Place For Photos - A place to tape, glue or staple pictures from you trips.

Vessel Information

Date of Purchase	From
Manufacturer	Model
Year Built	Hull#
Builder	Designer
Vessel Type	Class
Vertical Clearance	Hull Type

Engine Information

Manufacturer	Model
Serial # Port	Engine Oil Type
Serial # Starboard	Engine HP
Engine Oil Capacity	Battery Model
Cruising RPM	Max RPM
Vertical Clearance	Hull Type

Specification Information

Fuel Filter Mfg	Part #
Oil Filter Mfg	Part #
Spark Plug Brand	Part #
Water Pump Mfg	Part #
Impeller Kit Mfg	Part #

Generator Information

Manufacturer	Model #
Serial #	Install Date
Oil Type	Oil Capacity
Oil Filter	Fuel Filter
Impeller Kit Mfg	Part #

Expenditures Log

DATE	ITEM	PURCHASED FROM	PRICE

Expenditures Log

DATE	ITEM	PURCHASED FROM	PRICE

Expenditures Log

DATE	ITEM	PURCHASED FROM	PRICE

Expenditures Log

DATE	ITEM	PURCHASED FROM	PRICE

Expenditures Log

DATE	ITEM	PURCHASED FROM	PRICE

Boat Log Record

Date   Destination

Weather   Forecast

Wind   Visibility

Water Conditions   Length of Trip

My Crew

Passengers

Marinas/Ports Visited

Memories

The Day In Pictures

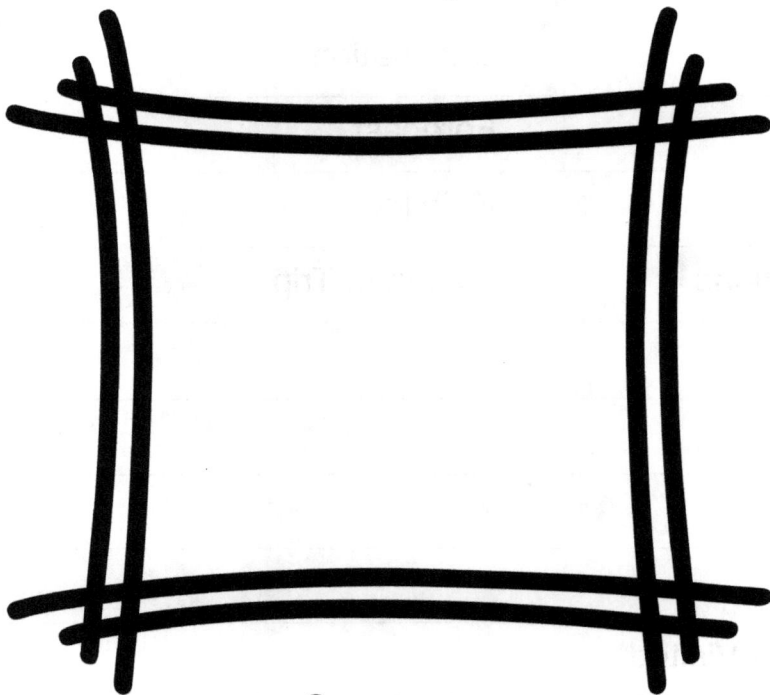

Boat Log Record

Date _____ Destination _____

Weather _____ Forecast _____

Wind _____ Visibility _____

Water Conditions _____ Length of Trip _____

My Crew _____

_____

Passengers _____

_____

Marinas/Ports Visited _____

Memories

_____

_____

_____

_____

_____

_____

_____

_____

The Day In Pictures

Boat Log Record

Date

Destination

Weather

Forecast

Wind

Visibility

Water Conditions

Length of Trip

My Crew

Passengers

Marinas/Ports Visited

Memories

The Day In Pictures

Boat Log Record

Date   Destination

Weather   Forecast

Wind   Visibility

Water Conditions   Length of Trip

My Crew

Passengers

Marinas/Ports Visited

Memories

The Day In Pictures

Boat Log Record

Date _____ Destination _____

Weather _____ Forecast _____

Wind _____ Visibility _____

Water Conditions _____ Length of Trip _____

My Crew _____

_____

Passengers _____

_____

Marinas/Ports Visited _____

Memories

_____

_____

_____

_____

_____

_____

_____

_____

The Day In Pictures

Boat Log Record

Date   Destination

Weather   Forecast

Wind   Visibility

Water Conditions   Length of Trip

My Crew

Passengers

Marinas/Ports Visited

Memories

The Day In Pictures

Boat Log Record

Date _____   Destination _____

Weather _____   Forecast _____

Wind _____   Visibility _____

Water Conditions _____   Length of Trip _____

My Crew _____

_____

Passengers _____

_____

Marinas/Ports Visited _____

Memories

_____

_____

_____

_____

_____

_____

_____

_____

_____

_____

_____

The Day In Pictures

Boat Log Record

Date   Destination

Weather   Forecast

Wind   Visibility

Water Conditions   Length of Trip

My Crew

Passengers

Marinas/Ports Visited

Memories

The Day In Pictures

Boat Log Record

Date _____ Destination _____

Weather _____ Forecast _____

Wind _____ Visibility _____

Water Conditions _____ Length of Trip _____

My Crew _____

_____

Passengers _____

_____

Marinas/Ports Visited _____

Memories

_____

_____

_____

_____

_____

_____

_____

_____

_____

The Day In Pictures

Boat Log Record

Date   Destination

Weather   Forecast

Wind   Visibility

Water Conditions   Length of Trip

My Crew

Passengers

Marinas/Ports Visited

Memories

The Day In Pictures

Boat Log Record

Date   Destination

Weather   Forecast

Wind   Visibility

Water Conditions   Length of Trip

My Crew

Passengers

Marinas/Ports Visited

Memories

The Day In Pictures

Boat Log Record

Date _____   Destination _____

Weather _____   Forecast _____

Wind _____   Visibility _____

Water Conditions _____   Length of Trip _____

My Crew _____

_____

Passengers _____

_____

Marinas/Ports Visited _____

Memories

_____

_____

_____

_____

_____

_____

_____

_____

_____

The Day In Pictures

Boat Log Record

Date   Destination

Weather   Forecast

Wind   Visibility

Water Conditions   Length of Trip

My Crew

Passengers

Marinas/Ports Visited

Memories

The Day In Pictures

Boat Log Record

Date _____ Destination _____

Weather _____ Forecast _____

Wind _____ Visibility _____

Water Conditions _____ Length of Trip _____

My Crew _____

_____

Passengers _____

_____

Marinas/Ports Visited _____

Memories

_____

_____

_____

_____

_____

_____

_____

_____

_____

The Day In Pictures

Boat Log Record

Date   Destination

Weather   Forecast

Wind   Visibility

Water Conditions   Length of Trip

My Crew

Passengers

Marinas/Ports Visited

Memories

The Day In Pictures

Boat Log Record

Date   Destination

Weather   Forecast

Wind   Visibility

Water Conditions   Length of Trip

My Crew

Passengers

Marinas/Ports Visited

Memories

The Day In Pictures

Boat Log Record

Date   Destination

Weather   Forecast

Wind   Visibility

Water Conditions   Length of Trip

My Crew

Passengers

Marinas/Ports Visited

Memories

The Day In Pictures

Boat Log Record

Date _____ Destination _____

Weather _____ Forecast _____

Wind _____ Visibility _____

Water Conditions _____ Length of Trip _____

My Crew _____

_____

Passengers _____

_____

Marinas/Ports Visited _____

Memories

_____

_____

_____

_____

_____

_____

_____

_____

The Day In Pictures

Boat Log Record

Date

Destination

Weather

Forecast

Wind

Visibility

Water Conditions

Length of Trip

My Crew

Passengers

Marinas/Ports Visited

Memories

The Day In Pictures

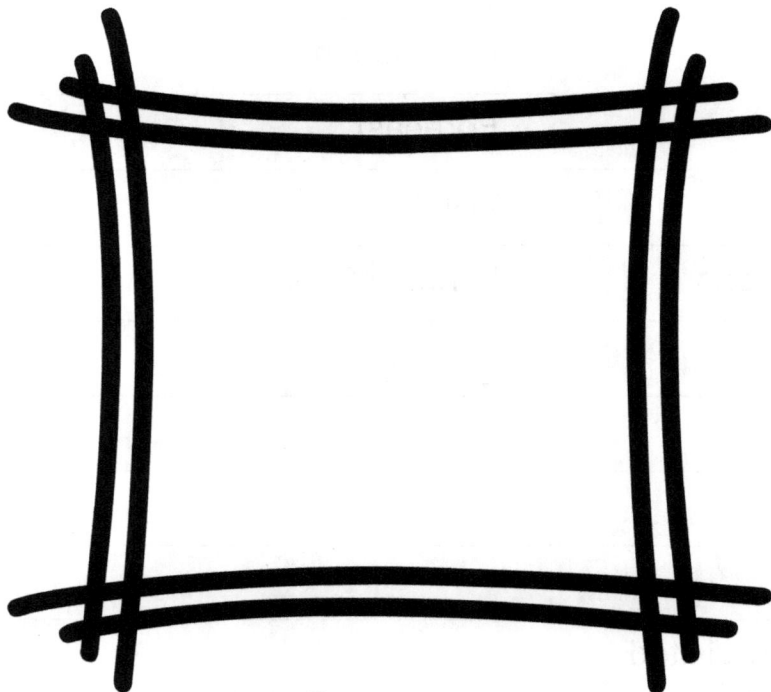

Boat Log Record

Date   Destination

Weather   Forecast

Wind   Visibility

Water Conditions   Length of Trip

My Crew

Passengers

Marinas/Ports Visited

Memories

The Day In Pictures

Boat Log Record

Date   Destination

Weather   Forecast

Wind   Visibility

Water Conditions   Length of Trip

My Crew

Passengers

Marinas/Ports Visited

Memories

The Day In Pictures

Boat Log Record

Date   Destination

Weather   Forecast

Wind   Visibility

Water Conditions   Length of Trip

My Crew

Passengers

Marinas/Ports Visited

Memories

The Day In Pictures

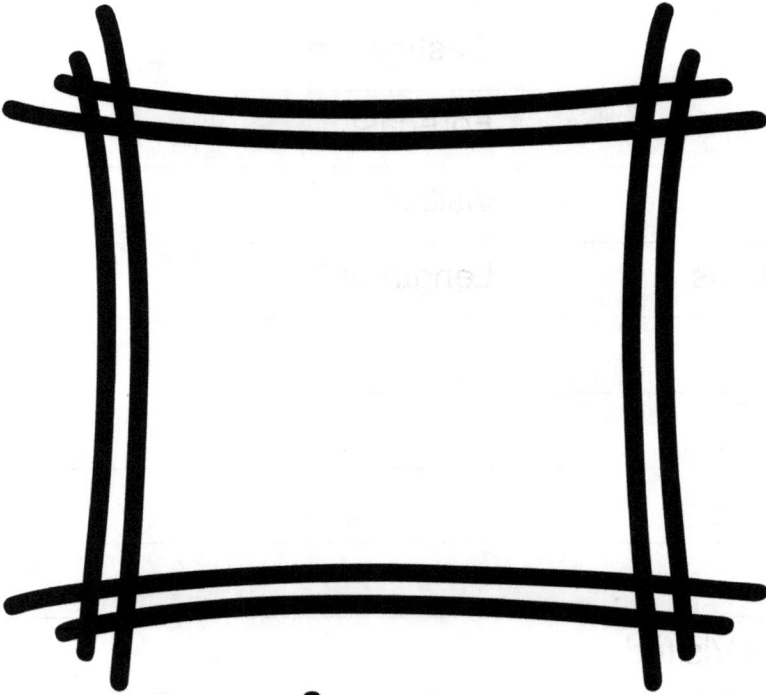

Boat Log Record

Date _____ Destination _____

Weather _____ Forecast _____

Wind _____ Visibility _____

Water Conditions _____ Length of Trip _____

My Crew _____

_____

Passengers _____

_____

Marinas/Ports Visited _____

Memories

_____

_____

_____

_____

_____

_____

_____

_____

_____

The Day In Pictures

Boat Log Record

Date _____ Destination _____

Weather _____ Forecast _____

Wind _____ Visibility _____

Water Conditions _____ Length of Trip _____

My Crew _____

_____

Passengers _____

_____

Marinas/Ports Visited _____

Memories

_____

_____

_____

_____

_____

_____

_____

_____

The Day In Pictures

Boat Log Record

Date _____ Destination _____

Weather _____ Forecast _____

Wind _____ Visibility _____

Water Conditions _____ Length of Trip _____

My Crew _____

_____

Passengers _____

_____

Marinas/Ports Visited _____

_____

Memories

_____

_____

_____

_____

_____

_____

_____

_____

The Day In Pictures

Boat Log Record

Date _____   Destination _____

Weather _____   Forecast _____

Wind _____   Visibility _____

Water Conditions _____   Length of Trip _____

My Crew _____

_____

Passengers _____

_____

Marinas/Ports Visited _____

Memories

_____

_____

_____

_____

_____

_____

_____

_____

_____

_____

The Day In Pictures

Boat Log Record

Date _____ Destination _____

Weather _____ Forecast _____

Wind _____ Visibility _____

Water Conditions _____ Length of Trip _____

My Crew _____

_____

Passengers _____

_____

Marinas/Ports Visited _____

Memories

_____

_____

_____

_____

_____

_____

_____

_____

The Day In Pictures

Boat Log Record

Date   Destination

Weather   Forecast

Wind   Visibility

Water Conditions   Length of Trip

My Crew

Passengers

Marinas/Ports Visited

Memories

The Day In Pictures

Boat Log Record

Date _____   Destination _____

Weather _____   Forecast _____

Wind _____   Visibility _____

Water Conditions _____   Length of Trip _____

My Crew _____

_____

Passengers _____

_____

Marinas/Ports Visited _____

Memories

_____

_____

_____

_____

_____

_____

_____

_____

_____

The Day In Pictures

Boat Log Record

Date   Destination

Weather   Forecast

Wind   Visibility

Water Conditions   Length of Trip

My Crew

Passengers

Marinas/Ports Visited

Memories

The Day In Pictures

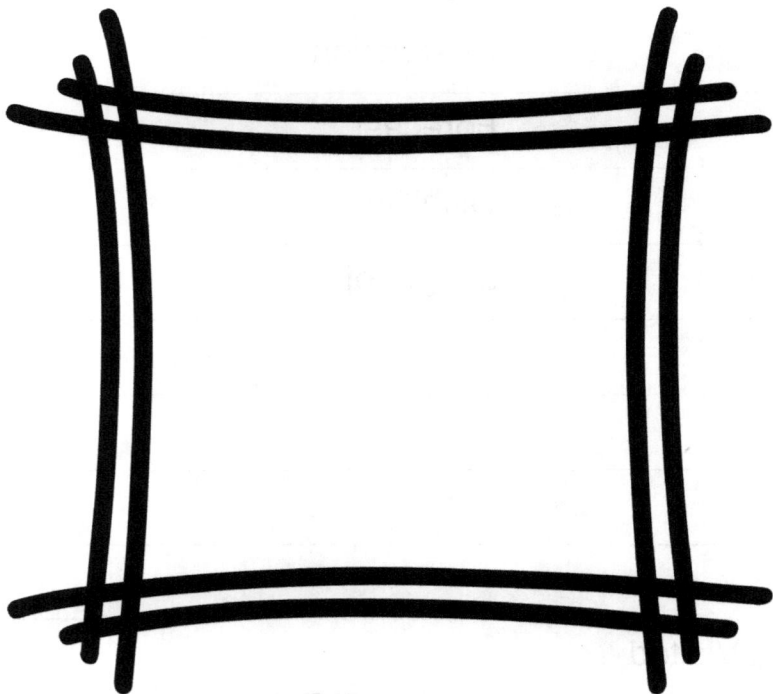

Boat Log Record

Date

Destination

Weather

Forecast

Wind

Visibility

Water Conditions

Length of Trip

My Crew

Passengers

Marinas/Ports Visited

Memories

The Day In Pictures

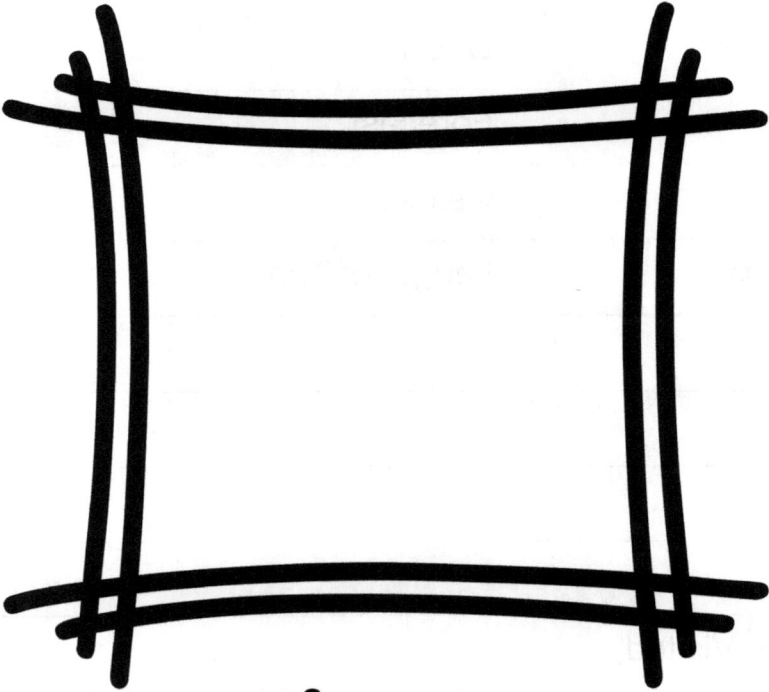

Boat Log Record

Date   Destination

Weather   Forecast

Wind   Visibility

Water Conditions   Length of Trip

My Crew

Passengers

Marinas/Ports Visited

Memories

The Day In Pictures

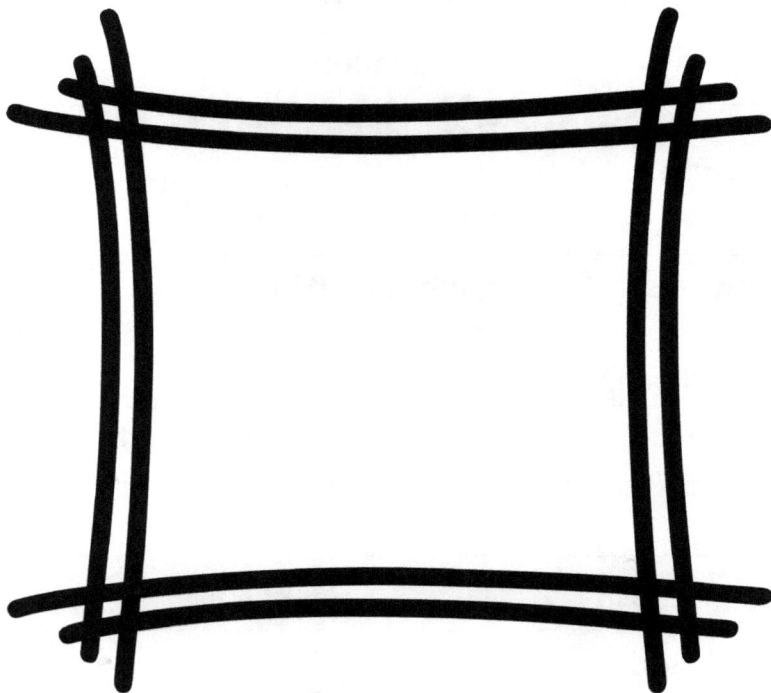

Boat Log Record

Date _____   Destination _____

Weather _____   Forecast _____

Wind _____   Visibility _____

Water Conditions _____   Length of Trip _____

My Crew _____

_____

Passengers _____

_____

Marinas/Ports Visited _____

Memories

_____

_____

_____

_____

_____

_____

_____

The Day In Pictures

Boat Log Record

Date   Destination

Weather   Forecast

Wind   Visibility

Water Conditions   Length of Trip

My Crew

Passengers

Marinas/Ports Visited

Memories

The Day In Pictures

Boat Log Record

Date _____ Destination _____

Weather _____ Forecast _____

Wind _____ Visibility _____

Water Conditions _____ Length of Trip _____

My Crew _____

_____

Passengers _____

_____

Marinas/Ports Visited _____

Memories

_____

_____

_____

_____

_____

_____

_____

_____

_____

_____

The Day In Pictures

Boat Log Record

Date _____ Destination _____

Weather _____ Forecast _____

Wind _____ Visibility _____

Water Conditions _____ Length of Trip _____

My Crew _____

_____

Passengers _____

_____

Marinas/Ports Visited _____

Memories

_____

_____

_____

_____

_____

_____

_____

_____

_____

The Day In Pictures

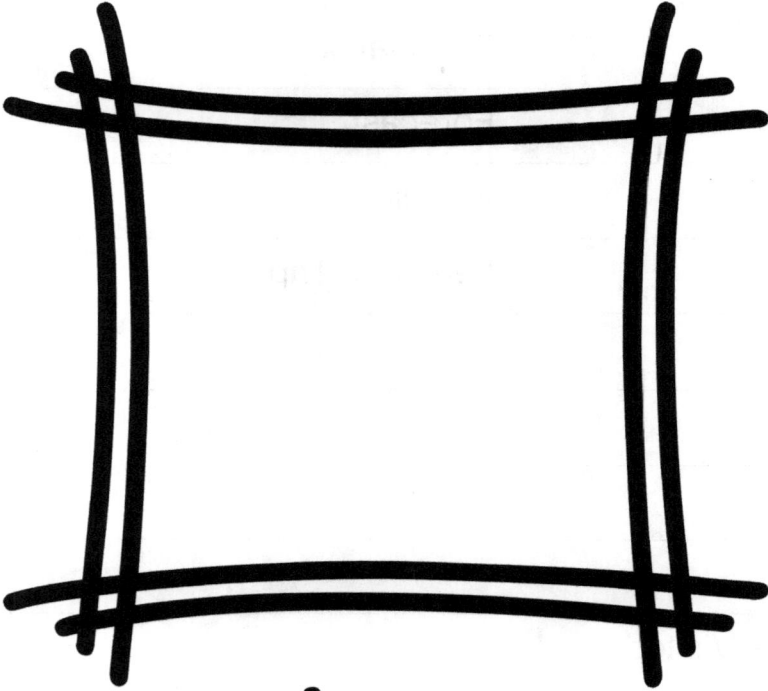

Boat Log Record

Date _____ Destination _____

Weather _____ Forecast _____

Wind _____ Visibility _____

Water Conditions _____ Length of Trip _____

My Crew _____

_____

Passengers _____

_____

Marinas/Ports Visited _____

Memories

_____

_____

_____

_____

_____

_____

_____

_____

The Day In Pictures

Boat Log Record

Date _____ Destination _____

Weather _____ Forecast _____

Wind _____ Visibility _____

Water Conditions _____ Length of Trip _____

My Crew _____

_____

Passengers _____

_____

Marinas/Ports Visited _____

Memories

_____

_____

_____

_____

_____

_____

_____

_____

The Day In Pictures

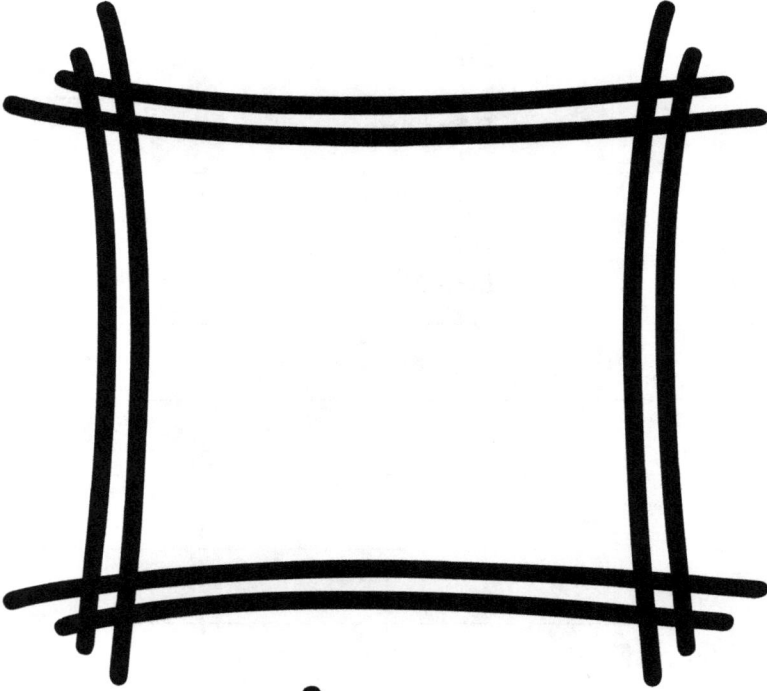

Boat Log Record

Date   Destination

Weather   Forecast

Wind   Visibility

Water Conditions   Length of Trip

My Crew

Passengers

Marinas/Ports Visited

Memories

The Day In Pictures

Boat Log Record

Date _____   Destination _____

Weather _____   Forecast _____

Wind _____   Visibility _____

Water Conditions _____   Length of Trip _____

My Crew _____

_____

_____

Passengers _____

_____

_____

Marinas/Ports Visited _____

_____

Memories

_____

_____

_____

_____

_____

_____

_____

_____

_____

The Day In Pictures

Boat Log Record

Date

Destination

Weather

Forecast

Wind

Visibility

Water Conditions

Length of Trip

My Crew

Passengers

Marinas/Ports Visited

Memories

The Day In Pictures

Boat Log Record

Date   Destination

Weather   Forecast

Wind   Visibility

Water Conditions   Length of Trip

My Crew

Passengers

Marinas/Ports Visited

Memories

The Day In Pictures

Boat Log Record

Date _____ Destination _____

Weather _____ Forecast _____

Wind _____ Visibility _____

Water Conditions _____ Length of Trip _____

My Crew _____

_____

Passengers _____

_____

Marinas/Ports Visited _____

Memories

_____

_____

_____

_____

_____

_____

_____

_____

The Day In Pictures

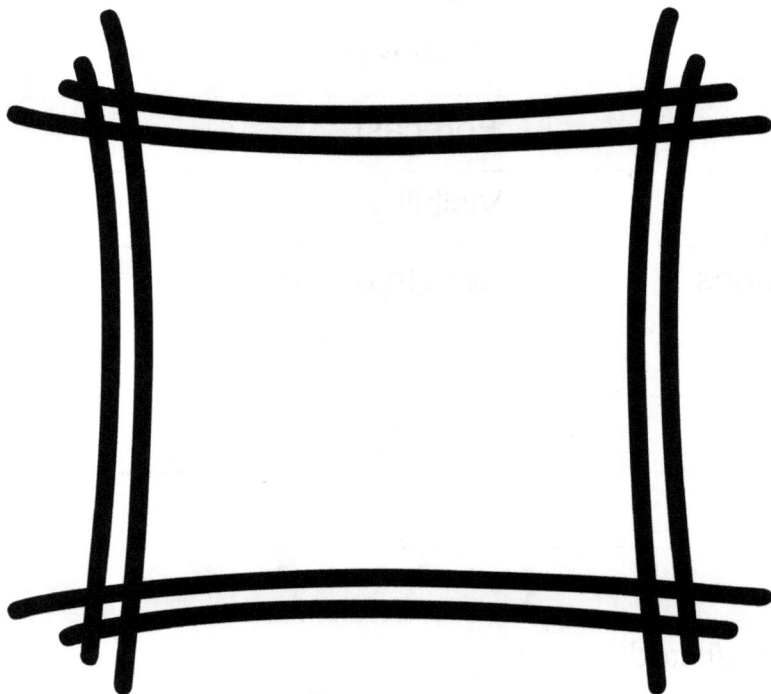

Boat Log Record

Date _____ Destination _____

Weather _____ Forecast _____

Wind _____ Visibility _____

Water Conditions _____ Length of Trip _____

My Crew _____

_____

Passengers _____

_____

Marinas/Ports Visited _____

Memories

_____

_____

_____

_____

_____

_____

_____

_____

_____

The Day In Pictures

Boat Log Record

Date

Destination

Weather

Forecast

Wind

Visibility

Water Conditions

Length of Trip

My Crew

Passengers

Marinas/Ports Visited

Memories

The Day In Pictures

Boat Log Record

Date _____   Destination _____

Weather _____   Forecast _____

Wind _____   Visibility _____

Water Conditions _____   Length of Trip _____

My Crew _____

_____

Passengers _____

_____

Marinas/Ports Visited _____

_____

Memories

_____

_____

_____

_____

_____

_____

_____

_____

_____

The Day In Pictures

Boat Log Record

Date   Destination

Weather   Forecast

Wind   Visibility

Water Conditions   Length of Trip

My Crew

Passengers

Marinas/Ports Visited

Memories

The Day In Pictures

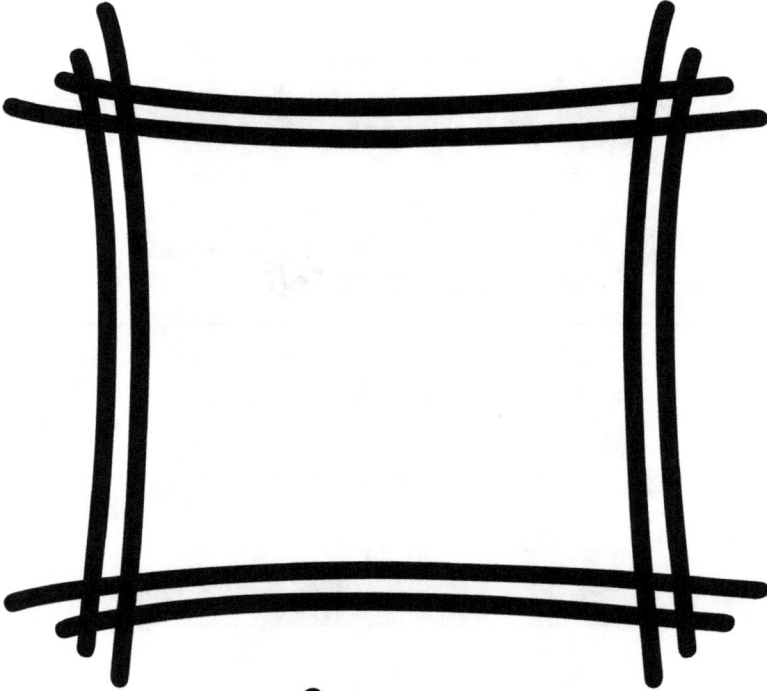

Boat Log Record

Date _____   Destination _____

Weather _____   Forecast _____

Wind _____   Visibility _____

Water Conditions _____   Length of Trip _____

My Crew _____

_____

Passengers _____

_____

Marinas/Ports Visited _____

_____

Memories

_____

_____

_____

_____

_____

_____

_____

_____

The Day In Pictures

Boat Log Record

Date   Destination

Weather   Forecast

Wind   Visibility

Water Conditions   Length of Trip

My Crew

Passengers

Marinas/Ports Visited

Memories

The Day In Pictures

Boat Log Record

Date _____ Destination _____

Weather _____ Forecast _____

Wind _____ Visibility _____

Water Conditions _____ Length of Trip _____

My Crew _____

_____

Passengers _____

_____

Marinas/Ports Visited _____

Memories

_____

_____

_____

_____

_____

_____

_____

_____

_____

The Day In Pictures

www.ingramcontent.com/pod-product-compliance
Lightning Source LLC
Chambersburg PA
CBHW051030030426
42336CB00015B/2801